The Step-By-Step Guide To
Pivot Tables
& Introduction To Dashboards

C.J. Benton

DEDICATION

To users who are searching for a concise
Microsoft® Excel® Pivot Tables and Dashboard book!

Other Books Available By This Author:

1. The **Step-By-Step** Guide To The 25 Most Common Microsoft® Excel® Formulas & Features

2. The **Step-By-Step** Guide To The **VLOOKUP** formula in Microsoft® Excel®

3. The Microsoft® Excel® **Step-By-Step** Training Guide **Book Bundle**

CONTENTS

CONTENTS

PREFACE

For nearly twenty years, I worked as a Data & Systems Analyst for three different Fortune 500 companies, primarily in the areas of Finance, Infrastructure Services, and Logistics. During that time I used Microsoft® Excel® extensively developing hundreds of different types of reports, analysis tools, and several forms of Dashboards.

I've utilized many Microsoft® Excel® features, including Pivot Tables. The following are the Pivot Table functions I used and taught the most to fellow colleagues.

.

INTRODUCTION

This book begins with a detailed review, with screenshots, of five basic and intermediate examples of Microsoft® Excel® Pivot Tables. Continuing with a tutorial on how to create a basic formatted Dashboard using Pivot Table data. Including a pie chart and instructions on updating a Dashboard with new or modified data. The next two chapters focus on supporting formulas. These formulas can be used as a helpful resource when troubleshooting Pivot Table reports, especially for those where the results are being displayed incorrectly. The book concludes with three examples of advanced Pivot Table functionality and a brief examination of some common Pivot Table error messages and how to resolve them.

CHAPTER 1
HOW TO USE THIS BOOK

This book can be used as a tutorial or quick reference guide. It is intended for users who are comfortable with the basics of Microsoft® Excel® and want to build upon this skill by learning Pivot Tables and Dashboards.

This book assumes you already know how to create, open, save, and modify an Excel® workbook and have a general familiarity with the Excel® toolbar.

All of the examples in this book use Microsoft® Excel® 2013, however most of the functionality and formulas can be applied with Microsoft® Excel® version 2007 or later.

While this book provides several basic, intermediate, and advanced Pivot Table examples, the book does not cover ALL available Microsoft® Excel® formulas and Pivot Table features and functionality.

Please always **back-up your work** and **save often**. A good best practice when attempting any new functionality is to **create a copy of the original spreadsheet** and implement your changes on the copied spreadsheet. Should anything go wrong, you then have the original spreadsheet to fall back on. Please see the diagram below.

Diagram 1:

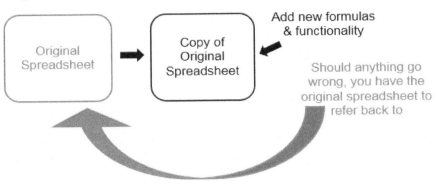

This book is structured to build on each previous chapter's teaching. Chapters 2, 3, & 4 cover the basic and intermediate features of Pivot Tables and Dashboards. Chapters 5 & 6 review supporting formulas that can be used when troubleshooting Pivot Table report results and other spreadsheets. The final chapters examine some advanced Pivot Table functionality and a few of the more common Pivot Table error messages and how to resolve them.

The below table is a summary of the functionality and features detailed in each chapter:

CHAPTER	FUNCTIONALITY / FEATURE(S)
Chapter 2 Pivot Table Basics	• Organizing & summarizing data • Formatting results • Inserting Pivot Charts • Displaying averages & percentages • Ranking data
Chapters 3 & 4 Dashboards	• How to create a basic Dashboard • Optional instructions for protecting Dashboard data and hiding tabs • Updating Pivot Table or Dashboard data, while keeping the existing formatting and presentation intact
Chapters 5 & 6 Supporting Formulas	• **LEN** - Counts the number of characters in a cell • **TRIM** - Removes all extraneous spaces from a cell, except for single spaces between words
Chapter 7 Pivot Tables Advanced	• Grouping data • Inserting calculated fields
Chapter 8 Pivot Table Error Messages	• Common Pivot Table error messages and how to resolve them

To enhance readability and for those who want to skip to specific areas, each chapter consists of *one or more* of the following sections:

Diagram 2:

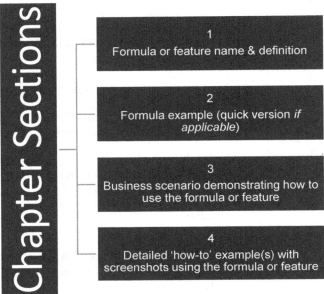

SECTION 1:
Provides the formula or feature name and definition for that chapter. *(Chapters 2, 5, & 6)*

SECTION 2:
Gives a quick example of how to use the formula and the results. This is intended for intermediate level users who do not require a detailed step-by-step example. Also, this section can be used as a quick reference of the syntax. *(Chapters 5 & 6)*

SECTION 3:
Offers one or more business scenarios demonstrating how the formula or feature may be used. *(Chapters 2 - 7)*

SECTION 4:
Presents detailed instructions with screenshots explaining how to answer each chapter's scenario questions or how to resolve common error messages. *(Chapters 2 - 8)*

CHAPTER 2
PIVOT TABLES (BASICS)

Feature:
- Pivot Tables

Definition:
- By using built-in filters and functions, Pivot Tables allow you to quickly organize and summarize large amounts of data. Various types of analysis can then be completed without needing to manually enter formulas into the spreadsheet you're analyzing.

Scenario:

You may be tasked with analyzing significant amounts of data, perhaps consisting of several thousand or hundreds of thousands of records, or you may have to reconcile information from many different sources and forms, such as assimilating material from:

1. Reports generated by another application, such as a legacy system

2. Data imported into Excel® via a query from a database or other application

3. Data copied or cut, and pasted into Excel® from the web or other types of screen scraping activities

One of the easiest ways to perform high level analysis on this information is to use Pivot Tables. The following examples will demonstrate five types of analysis that can be performed on large amounts of data using the Microsoft® Excel® Pivot Table feature. In the following examples we will:

1. Determine the total sales by region and quarter

2. Create a chart that displays the sales by region and quarter

3. Show the individual fruit sales by region and quarter

4. Identify what the percentage of individual fruit sales are by quarter and what the overall percentage of total sales are for each region

5. Rank each sales person, including their total & average sales

Sample data for examples 1- 5 above, due to space limitations **the entire data set is not displayed**.

To download a free copy of the Excel® file used in this scenario please go to:
http://bentonexcelbooks.my-free.website/sample-data-files
select the file for Chapter 2 (Pivot Tables) in the 'The Step-By-Step Guide To Pivot Tables & Introduction to Dashboards' section.

	A	B	C	D	E	F	G	H	I
1	REGION	SALES PERSON FIRST NAME	SALES PERSON LAST NAME	SALES PERSON ID	QUARTER	APPLES	ORANGES	MANGOS	TOTAL
2	Central	bob	TAYLOR	1174	1	1,810	2,039	1,771	5,620
3	Central	helen	SMITH	833	1	102	354	59	516
4	Central	jill	JOHNSON	200	1	93	322	54	469
5	Central	sally	MORTON	500	1	595	824	556	1,975
6	Central	sam	BECKER	800	1	863	1,092	824	2,779
7	East	Abbey	Williams	690	1	346	237	260	843
8	East	John	Dower	255	1	260	178	195	633
9	East	John	Wilson	300	1	286	196	215	696
10	East	Mary	Nelson	600	1	315	215	236	766
11	East	Sarah	Taylor	900	1	381	261	285	927
12	West	Alex	Steller	1000	1	163	212	127	502
13	West	Billy	Winchester	1156	1	179	234	140	552
14	West	Helen	Simpson	817	1	148	193	116	457
15	West	Jack	Smith	100	1	111	145	87	343
16	West	Joe	Tanner	400	1	122	160	96	377
17	West	Peter	Graham	700	1	134	175	105	415
18	Central	bob	TAYLOR	1174	2	113	390	65	567
19	Central	helen	SMITH	833	2	1,006	1,393	940	3,338
20	Central	jill	JOHNSON	200	2	774	1,071	723	2,568
21	Central	sally	MORTON	500	2	1,295	1,638	1,236	4,169
22	Central	sam	BECKER	800	2	2,806	3,160	2,745	8,711
23	East	Abbey	Williams	690	2	1,674	1,494	1,531	4,699
24	East	John	Dower	255	2	762	680	697	2,139

Detailed Example How To Use The Feature:

Let's first determine the '**Total Sales by Region**' and then we will

build upon this by adding the '**Quarterly Sales by Region**':

1. In this example, **cells A1:I65** were selected

2. From the toolbar select **INSERT : PivotTable**

The following dialogue box should appear:

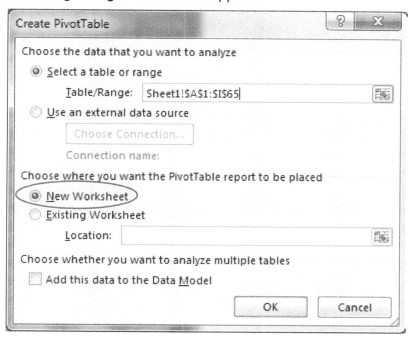

3. For this demonstration, the '**New Worksheet**' radio button has been selected

4. Click the '**OK**' button

A new tab will be created and looks similar to the following *(due to display limitations the below screenshot is split, showing the left & right sides of your screen separately)*:

Left side of your screen:

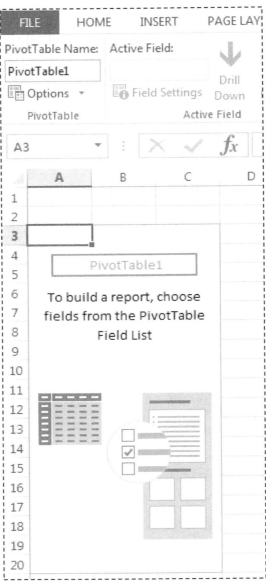

Right side of your screen:

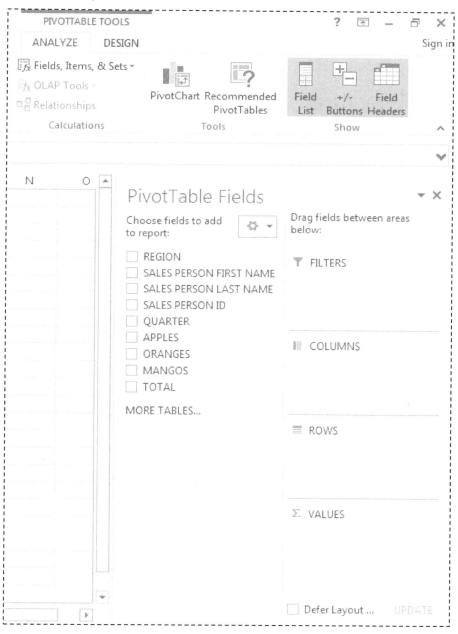

5. Click the **'REGION'** and **'TOTAL' PivotTable Field** check boxes

The following should be displayed on the left side of your screen
Note: the format is not very easy to read.

	A	B
1		
2		
3	Row Labels ▾	Sum of TOTAL
4	Central	138571.3795
5	East	145587.9689
6	West	196786.7115
7	Grand Total	480946.0598

6. We can change the column labels and format of the numbers. In the below example:

   a. Cell label **'A3'** was changed to **'REGION'**

   b. Cell label **'B3'** was changed to **'TOTAL SALES'**

   c. The dollar sales total format was changed to currency with zero decimal places

Below is the formatted example:

	A	B
1		
2		
3	REGION ▾	TOTALS SALES
4	Central	$ 138,571
5	East	$ 145,588
6	West	$ 196,787
7	Grand Total	$ 480,946

7. Now let's add the **'QUARTER'** by clicking the check box labeled **'QUARTER'** from the **PivotTable Fields** list. *Note: you may also drag the field 'QUARTER' over to the 'COLUMNS' section of the PivotTable Fields list.*

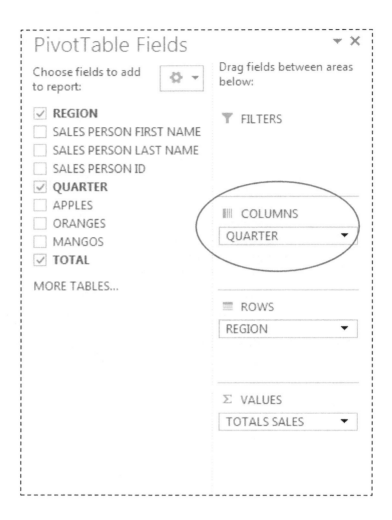

We now have **'QUARTER'** added to the summary

8. The label for cell **'B3'** was changed to **'BY QUARTER'**

9. The labels for cells **'B4'**, **'C4'**, **'D4'**, & **'E4'** were changed by adding the abbreviation '**QTR**' in front of each quarter number

Before *formatting:*

	A	B	C	D	E	F
1						
2						
3	TOTALS SALES	Column Labels ▼				
4	REGION ▼		1	2	3	4 Grand Total
5	Central	$	11,359	$19,352	$ 34,097	$ 73,763 $ 138,571
6	East	$	3,865	$19,343	$ 38,811	$ 83,569 $ 145,588
7	West	$	2,646	$23,586	$ 42,590	$127,964 $ 196,787
8	Grand Total	$	17,870	$62,281	$115,499	$285,296 $ 480,946

After *formatting:*

	TOTALS SALES	BY QUARTER ▼	QTR 2	QTR 3	QTR 4	Grand Total
3	TOTALS SALES	BY QUARTER ▼				
4	REGION ▼	QTR 1	QTR 2	QTR 3	QTR 4	Grand Total
5	Central	$ 11,359	$19,352	$ 34,097	$ 73,763	$ 138,571
6	East	$ 3,865	$19,343	$ 38,811	$ 83,569	$ 145,588
7	West	$ 2,646	$23,586	$ 42,590	$127,964	$ 196,787
8	Grand Total	$ 17,870	$62,281	$115,499	$285,296	$ 480,946

Now that we have determined the '**Total Sales by Region**' and the '**Quarterly Sales by Region,**' let's add a chart to the summary

1. From the PIVOTTABLE TOOLS toolbar select the tab **ANALYZE : PivotChart**

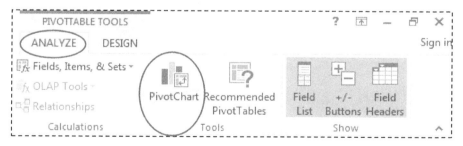

Note: *If you do not see the PIVOTTABLE TOOLS option on your toolbar, click any PivotTable cell. This toolbar option only appears when a PivotTable field is active.*

The following dialogue box should appear:

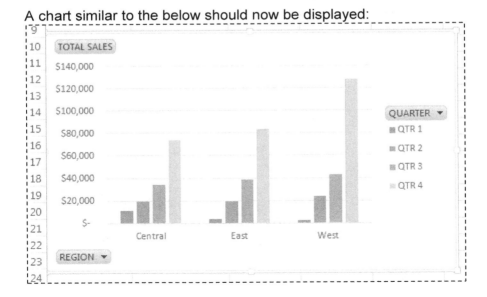

2. Click the **'OK'** button

A chart similar to the below should now be displayed:

Note: for the remainder of this chapter's Pivot Table examples we do not need the chart. Please delete the chart by clicking on the chart and pressing the delete button on your keyboard.

Next, we'll extend our analysis by adding the individual fruit sales to our summary.

1. Drag the **'QUARTER'** field from the **'COLUMNS'** section to the **'ROWS'** section.

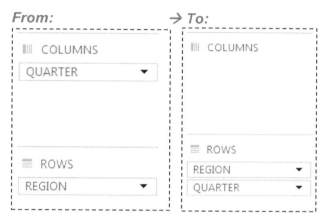

The PivotTable Fields box should now appear as follows:

2. Drag the fields **'APPLES'**, '**ORANGES**', & **'MANGOS'** to the **'VALUES'** section of the **PivotTables Fields** list

The results should look similar to the following:

	A	B	C	D	E
1					
2					
3	REGION ▾	TOTAL APPLES	TOTAL ORANGES	TOTAL MANGOS	TOTAL SALES
4	⊟ Central	$ 43,481	$ 53,278	$ 41,812	$ 138,571
5	QTR 1	$ 3,463	$ 4,631	$ 3,264	$ 11,359
6	QTR 2	$ 5,992	$ 7,652	$ 5,709	$ 19,352
7	QTR 3	$ 10,634	$ 13,280	$ 10,183	$ 34,097
8	QTR 4	$ 23,392	$ 27,715	$ 22,656	$ 73,763
9	⊟ East	$ 50,626	$ 47,117	$ 47,845	$ 145,588
10	QTR 1	$ 1,587	$ 1,087	$ 1,190	$ 3,865
11	QTR 2	$ 6,891	$ 6,149	$ 6,303	$ 19,343
12	QTR 3	$ 13,583	$ 12,502	$ 12,726	$ 38,811
13	QTR 4	$ 28,564	$ 27,380	$ 27,625	$ 83,569
14	⊟ West	$ 69,750	$ 65,259	$ 61,778	$ 196,787
15	QTR 1	$ 856	$ 1,119	$ 671	$ 2,646
16	QTR 2	$ 7,819	$ 8,253	$ 7,513	$ 23,586
17	QTR 3	$ 15,335	$ 14,074	$ 13,182	$ 42,590
18	QTR 4	$ 45,739	$ 41,813	$ 40,411	$ 127,964
19	Grand Total	$ 163,857	$ 165,655	$ 151,435	$ 480,946

We covered some of the basic types of analysis that we can do with Pivot Tables, now let's go a few steps further by answering the following questions.

- What is the percentage of Individual Fruit Sales by Quarter?
- What is the percentage of Total Sales for each Region?

1. Uncheck (deselect) the **'TOTAL SALES'** & **'REGION'** boxes from the Pivot 'Field List'

Row Labels	Sum of APPLES	Sum of ORANGES	Sum of MANGOS	Sum of TOTAL
Central	$ 43,481	$ 53,278	$ 41,812	$ 138,571
1	$ 3,463	$ 4,631	$ 3,264	$ 11,359
2	$ 5,992	$ 7,652	$ 5,709	$ 19,352
3	$ 10,634	$ 13,280	$ 10,183	$ 34,097
4	$ 23,392	$ 27,715	$ 22,656	$ 73,763
East	$ 50,626	$ 47,117	$ 47,845	$ 145,588
1	$ 1,587	$ 1,087	$ 1,190	$ 3,865
2	$ 6,891	$ 6,149	$ 6,303	$ 19,343
3	$ 13,583	$ 12,502	$ 12,726	$ 38,811
4	$ 28,564	$ 27,380	$ 27,625	$ 83,569
West	$ 69,750	$ 65,259	$ 61,778	$ 196,787
1	$ 856	$ 1,119	$ 671	$ 2,646
2	$ 7,819	$ 8,253	$ 7,513	$ 23,586
3	$ 15,335	$ 14,074	$ 13,182	$ 42,590
4	$ 45,739	$ 41,813	$ 40,411	$ 127,964
Grand Total	$ 163,857	$ 165,655	$ 151,435	$ 480,946

Only the following fields should be selected:

2. Click on the **'Sum of APPLES'** drop-down box and select **'Value Field Settings...'**.

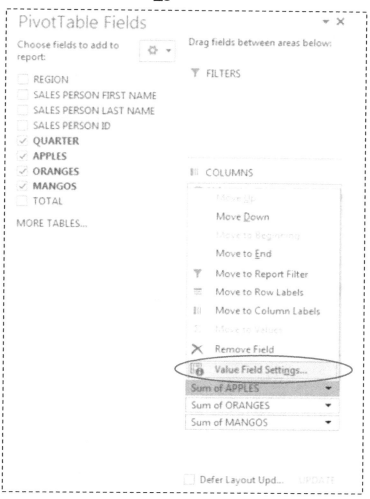

The following dialogue box should appear:

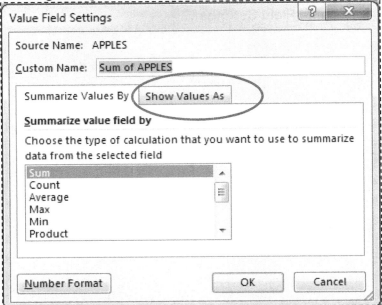

3. Select the tab **'Show Values As'**

4. From the '**Show values as**' drop-down list select '**% of Grand Total**'

5. Click the '**OK**' button

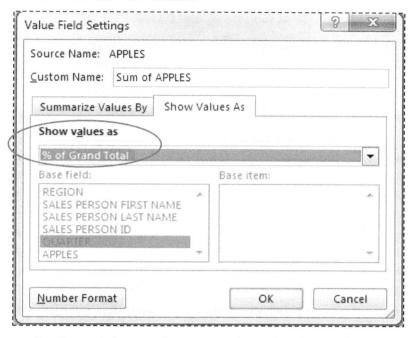

6. Repeat the previous steps 2 - 5 for '**Sum of ORANGES**' and '**Sum of MANGOS**'

The Totals by fruit have been changed to a percentage. ***Note: the column labels have been changed and the number of decimal places reduced for the percentages***

	QUARTER ▼	% of APPLES	% of ORANGES	% of MANGOS
3				
4	QTR 1	4%	4%	3%
5	QTR 2	13%	13%	13%
6	QTR 3	24%	24%	24%
7	QTR 4	60%	59%	60%
8	Grand Total	100%	100%	100%

Please note: In Excel®, often the percentages when summed together may exceed or not equal 100%, this is due to Excel® rounding the percentages either up or down.

We've now answered the question, what are the percentage of Individual Fruit Sales by Quarter

To determine the percentage of Total Sales for each Region

7. Remove (uncheck) the fields **'APPLES,' 'ORANGES,' 'MANGOS,'** and **'QUARTER'**

8. Add the **'TOTAL'** field

See the below **PivotTable Fields** list:

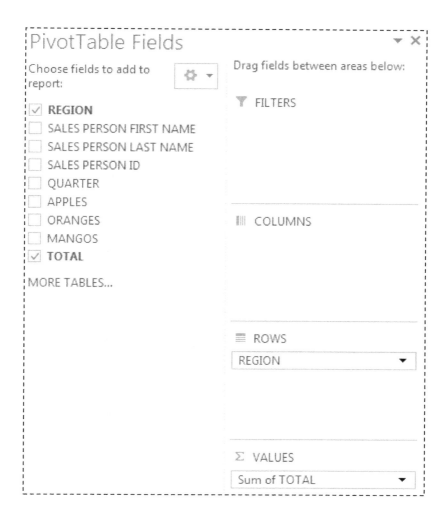

9. Click on the **'Sum of TOTAL'** drop-down box and select **'Value Field Settings…'**.

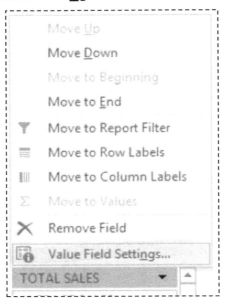

The following dialogue box should appear:

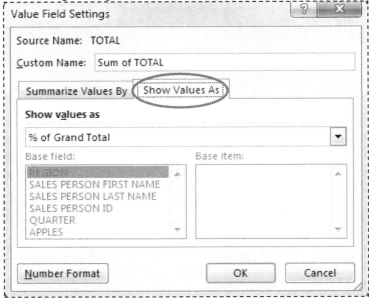

10. Select the tab **'Show Values As'**

11. From the **'Show values as'** drop-down list select **'% of Grand Total'**

12. Click the **'OK'** button

We've now determined the percentage of Total Sales for each Region.

3	REGION ▼	Sum of TOTAL
4	Central	28.81%
5	East	30.27%
6	West	40.92%
7	**Grand Total**	**100.00%**

All of the previous Pivot Table examples focused on *summary level* types of analysis, now let's take a look at some individual results by:

- Ranking each Sales Person, including their Total & Average Sales

Create a new Pivot Table using similar sample data as above.

1. Begin by selecting the **'SALES PERSON ID'** and adding the **'TOTAL'** field *three* times to the **'VALUES'** section.

The spreadsheet will look *similar* to the below. *Note: all three of the 'Sum of TOTAL' columns are currently the same. We will be changing them in the following steps.*

	A	B	C	D
1				
2				
3	Row Labels ▾	Sum of TOTAL	Sum of TOTAL2	Sum of TOTAL3
4	100	10339	10339	10339
5	200	30217.4275	30217.4275	30217.4275
6	255	11499	11499	11499
7	300	16856.7	16856.7	16856.7
8	400	15276.2	15276.2	15276.2
9	500	20332.2129	20332.2129	20332.2129
10	600	24898.65	24898.65	24898.65
11	690	37013.424	37013.424	37013.424
12	700	22708.425	22708.425	22708.425
13	800	17755.0365	17755.0365	17755.0365
14	817	33931.63025	33931.63025	33931.63025
15	833	45671.45013	45671.45013	45671.45013
16	900	55320.19485	55320.19485	55320.19485
17	1000	50925.33004	50925.33004	50925.33004
18	1156	63606.12616	63606.12616	63606.12616
19	1174	24595.2525	24595.2525	24595.2525
20	Grand Total	480946.0598	480946.0598	480946.0598

2. Change the label for cell '**A3**' to '**SALES PERSON ID**'

3. Change the label for cell '**B3**' to '**TOTAL SALES**'

4. Change the label for cell '**C3**' to '**AVERAGE SALES**'

5. Change the label for cell '**D3**' to '**RANK**'

6. Change the formatting for columns '**B**' & '**C**' to currency with zero decimal places

7. In the **PivotTable Fields** list, in the **'VALUES'** section, click the drop-down box for **'AVERAGE SALES'**

8. Select the **'Value Field Settings…'** option

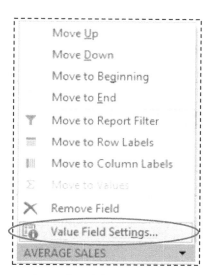

The following dialogue box should appear:

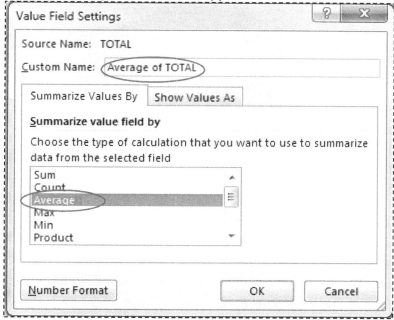

9. From the '**Summarize value field by**' list select '**Average**'. *Note: this will change the* '***Custom Name:***' *to* '***Average of TOTAL***', *change back to* '**AVERAGE SALES**'

10. Click the '**OK**' button

Next, change the field **'RANK'**

> 11. In the **PivotTable Fields** list, in the **'VALUES'** section, select the drop-down box for **'RANK'**
>
> 12. Select the **'Value Field Settings...'** option

The following dialogue box should appear:

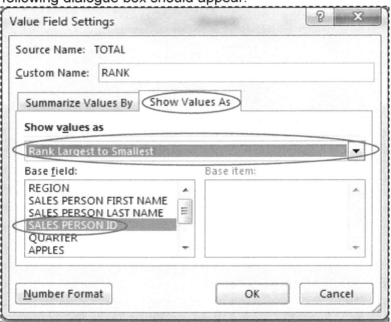

> 13. Select the tab **'Show Values As'**
>
> 14. From the **'Show values as'** drop-down list select **'Rank Largest to Smallest'**
>
> 15. For the **'Base field:'** box select **'SALES PERSON ID'**
>
> 16. Click the **'OK'** button

*The results should look **similar** to the following:*

3	SALES PERSON ID ▼	TOTAL SALES	AVERAGE SALES	RANK
4	100	$ 10,339	$ 2,585	16
5	200	$ 30,217	$ 7,554	7
6	255	$ 11,499	$ 2,875	15
7	300	$ 16,857	$ 4,214	13
8	400	$ 15,276	$ 3,819	14
9	500	$ 20,332	$ 5,083	11
10	600	$ 24,899	$ 6,225	8
11	690	$ 37,013	$ 9,253	5
12	700	$ 22,708	$ 5,677	10
13	800	$ 17,755	$ 4,439	12
14	817	$ 33,932	$ 8,483	6
15	833	$ 45,671	$ 11,418	4
16	900	$ 55,320	$ 13,830	2
17	1000	$ 50,925	$ 12,731	3
18	1156	$ 63,606	$ 15,902	1
19	1174	$ 24,595	$ 6,149	9
20	**Grand Total**	**$ 480,946**	**$ 7,515**	

Let's improve the readability:

17. With your cursor in cell **'A3'** from the toolbar select PIVOTTABLE TOOLS and the tab **DESIGN**

18. Check the box **'Banded Rows'**

19. Place your cursor in cell **'A3'** and click the drop-down arrow

20. Select the option called **'More Sort Options…'**

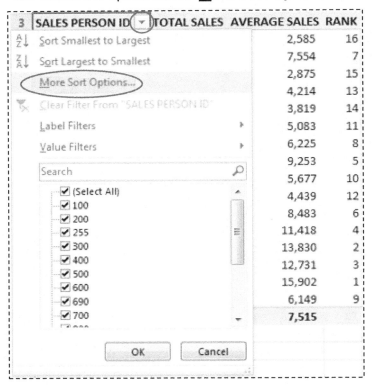

The following dialogue box will appear:

21. Select the '**Descending (Z to A) by:**' radio button

22. Select '**RANK**' from the drop-down box

23. Click the '**OK**' button

We now have a nicely formatted report that shows us each Sales Person's sales rank and their Total and Average Sales.

3	SALES PERSON ID ↴	TOTAL SALES	AVERAGE SALES	RANK
4	1156	$ 63,606	$ 15,902	1
5	900	$ 55,320	$ 13,830	2
6	1000	$ 50,925	$ 12,731	3
7	833	$ 45,671	$ 11,418	4
8	690	$ 37,013	$ 9,253	5
9	817	$ 33,932	$ 8,483	6
10	200	$ 30,217	$ 7,554	7
11	600	$ 24,899	$ 6,225	8
12	1174	$ 24,595	$ 6,149	9
13	700	$ 22,708	$ 5,677	10
14	500	$ 20,332	$ 5,083	11
15	800	$ 17,755	$ 4,439	12
16	300	$ 16,857	$ 4,214	13
17	400	$ 15,276	$ 3,819	14
18	255	$ 11,499	$ 2,875	15
19	100	$ 10,339	$ 2,585	16
20	Grand Total	$ 480,946	$ 7,515	

- For advanced Pivot Table examples, please see **Chapter 7**.
- For troubleshooting suggestions, please see **Chapter 8**.

CHAPTER 3
INTRODUCTION TO DASHBOARDS

In the previous examples, we added one Pivot Table per spreadsheet tab, in this chapter we will demonstrate how to add more than one Pivot Table to a tab, with tips on creating and formatting a basic Dashboard.

In chapter 4, we will illustrate how to update (Refresh) data once you have a Pivot Table or Dashboard formatted in a preferred layout.

Scenario:
You've been asked to create a monthly sales Dashboard that shows the following:

1. Total fruit sales by region and month
2. Individual fruits sales by region
3. Total fruit sales by region
4. A pie chart with the percent of total sales by region

The data is generated from a database query. You'll receive a new report at the start of every month of the prior month's sales results.

Detailed Example How To Use The Feature:
Sample data to create a basic Dashboard **_Note:_** *the sample contains only _four months of data_, but in the design we will plan for _twelve months_ so the Dashboard can be easily updated.*

To download a free copy of the Excel® file used in this scenario please go to:
http://bentonexcelbooks.my-free.website/sample-data-files
select the file for Chapter 3 (Dashboards) in the 'The Step-By-Step Guide To Pivot Tables & Introduction to Dashboards' section.

	A	B	C	D	E	F
1	REGION	MONTH	APPLES	ORANGES	MANGOS	TOTAL
2	Central	January	$3,463	$4,631	$3,264	$11,359
3	Central	February	$5,992	$7,652	$5,709	$19,352
4	Central	March	$10,634	$13,280	$10,183	$34,097
5	Central	April	$23,392	$27,715	$22,656	$73,763
6	East	January	$1,587	$1,087	$1,190	$3,865
7	East	February	$6,891	$6,149	$6,303	$19,343
8	East	March	$13,583	$12,502	$12,726	$38,811
9	East	April	$28,564	$27,380	$27,625	$83,569
10	West	January	$722	$943	$566	$2,231
11	West	February	$6,121	$6,494	$5,857	$18,472
12	West	March	$13,864	$12,577	$11,729	$38,170
13	West	April	$39,990	$36,023	$34,691	$110,704

1. Create a new Pivot Table, please see the beginning of chapter 2, if you do not already know how to create a Pivot Table.

Please select **columns 'A' – 'F'** for your **Table/Range**.

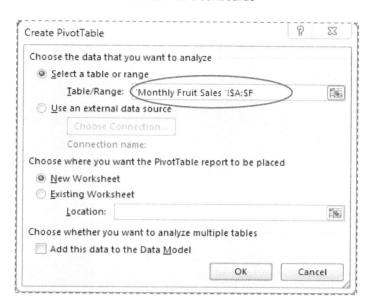

2. Rename the tab from **'Sheet2'** to **'Dashboard'**

From:

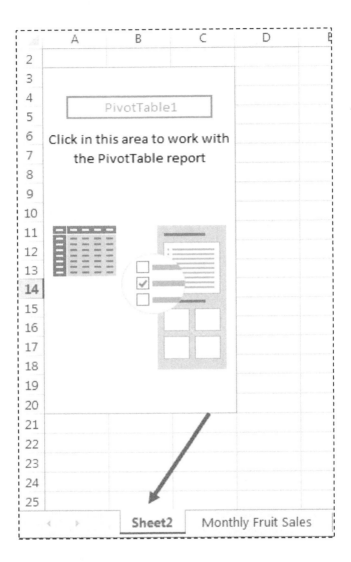

To:

3. We'll begin by adding the Total fruit sales by region and month

4. The PivotTable Fields selected are:
   a. COLUMNS = MONTH
   b. ROWS = REGION
   c. VALUES = Sum of TOTAL

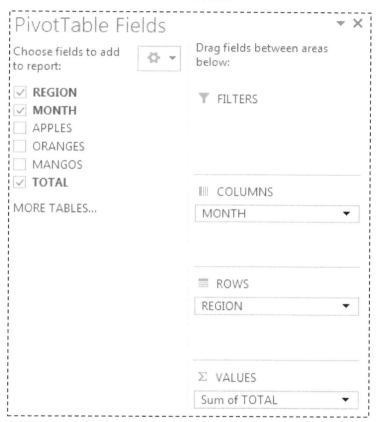

The following should be our results:

Sum of TOTAL	Column Labels					
Row Labels	January	February	March	April	(blank)	Grand Total
Central	11358.9	19352.24	34097.239	73763.00053		138571.3795
East	3864.5283	19343.1909	38810.8125	83569.43715		145587.9689
West	2231.42423	18472.41947	38170.24125	110703.5915		169577.6765
(blank)						
Grand Total	17454.85253	57167.85037	111078.2928	268036.0292		453737.0248

5. Next, we will add Individual fruits sales by region
6. Go back to our sample data (the tab **Monthly Fruit Sales**)
7. From the toolbar select **INSERT**: **PivotTable**
8. When you receive the **Create PivotTable** prompt, select the '**Existing Worksheet**' radio button
9. Place your cursor inside the '**Location:**' box

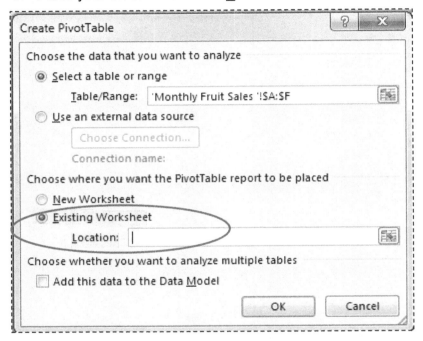

10. With your cursor still inside the '**Location:**' box click the '**Dashboard**' tab and then cell '**A11**'

11. The '**Location:**' box should now have **Dashboard!$A$11** entered

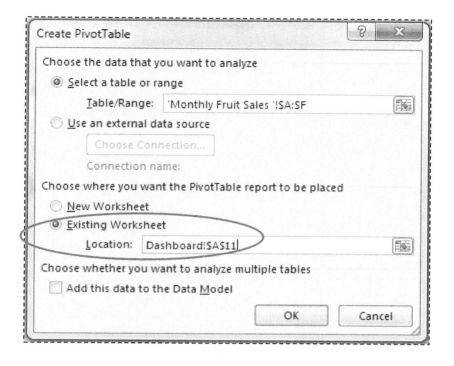

12. Click the 'OK' button

Your screen should look similar to the following:

13. The fields selected for the *second* Pivot Table are:
```
a. ROWS = REGION
b. VALUES =  Sum of APPLES
             Sum of ORANGES
             Sum of MANGOS
             Sum of TOTAL
```

PivotTable Fields   ▼ ✕

Choose fields to add to report: ⚙ ▼

Drag fields between areas below:

☑ **REGION**
☐ MONTH
☑ **APPLES**
☑ **ORANGES**
☑ **MANGOS**
☑ **TOTAL**

MORE TABLES...

▼ FILTERS

▥ COLUMNS

Σ Values	▼

≡ ROWS

REGION	▼

Σ VALUES

Sum of APPLES	▼
Sum of ORANGES	▼
Sum of MANGOS	▼
Sum of TOTAL	▼

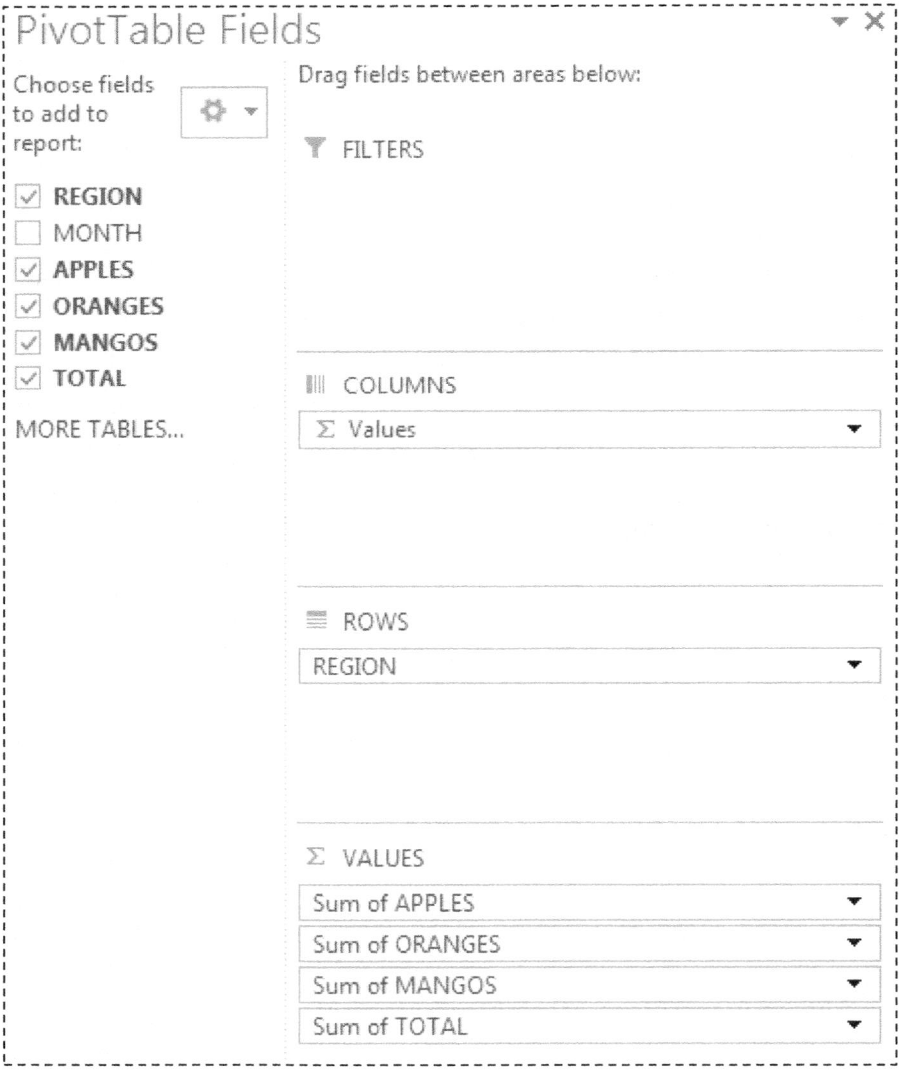

Your screen should look similar to the following:

Row Labels ▾	January	February	March	April	(blank)	Grand Total
Central	11358.9	19352.24	34097.239	73763.00053		138571.3795
East	3864.5283	19343.1909	38810.8125	83569.43715		145587.9689
West	2231.42423	18472.41947	38170.24125	110703.5915		169577.6765
(blank)						
Grand Total	17454.85253	57167.85037	111078.2928	268036.0292		453737.0248

Row Labels ▾	Sum of APPLES	Sum of ORANGES	Sum of MANGOS	Sum of TOTAL
Central	43480.80136	53278.35597	41812.22219	138571.3795
East	50625.74293	47117.44827	47844.77765	145587.9689
West	60697.03378	56037.4377	52843.20497	169577.6765
(blank)				
Grand Total	154803.5781	156433.2419	142500.2048	453737.0248

Next, well add the total fruit sales by region

14. Go back to our sample data (the tab **Monthly Fruit Sales**)

15. From the toolbar select **INSERT**: **PivotTable**

16. When you receive the **Create PivotTable** prompt, select the **'Existing Worksheet'** radio button

17. Place your cursor inside the **'Location:'** box

18. With your cursor still inside the **'Location:'** box click the **'Dashboard'** tab and then cell **'G11'**

19. The **'Location:'** box should now have **Dashboard!$G$11** entered

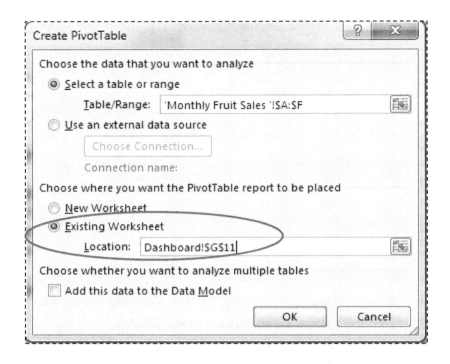

20. Click the **'OK'** button

21. The fields selected for the *third* Pivot Table are:
```
a. ROWS = REGION
b. VALUES = Sum of TOTAL
```

Your screen should look similar to the following:

Row Labels ▾	January	February	March	April	(blank)	Grand Total
Central	11358.9	19352.24	34097.239	73763.00053		138571.3795
East	3864.5283	19343.1909	38810.8125	83569.43715		145587.9689
West	2231.42423	18472.41947	38170.24125	110703.5915		169577.6765
(blank)						
Grand Total	17454.85253	57167.85037	111078.2928	268036.0292		453737.0248

Row Labels ▾	Sum of APPLES	Sum of ORANGES	Sum of MANGOS	Sum of TOTAL		Row Labels ▾	Sum of TOTAL
Central	43480.80136	53278.35597	41812.22219	138571.3795		Central	138571.3795
East	50625.74293	47117.44827	47844.77765	145587.9689		East	145587.9689
West	60697.03378	56037.4377	52843.20497	169577.6765		West	169577.6765
(blank)						(blank)	
Grand Total	154803.5781	156433.2419	142500.2048	453737.0248		Grand Total	453737.0248

22. Lastly, we will add the pie chart with the percent of total sales by region

23. Click cell **'G12'** on the **Dashboard tab**

24. From the PIVOTTABLE TOOLS toolbar select the tab **ANALYZE : PivotChart**

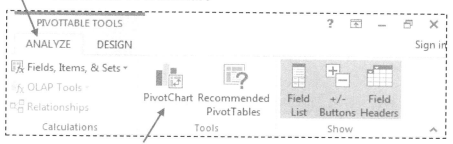

The following dialogue box should appear:

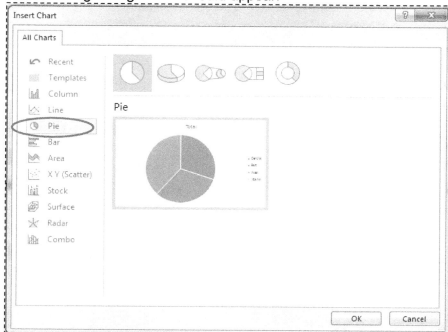

25. Select the **'Pie'** option

26. Click the **'OK'** button

The following pie chart should now be displayed *(you may need to drag you chart down near cell 'A18')*. We will add the percentages in a later step.

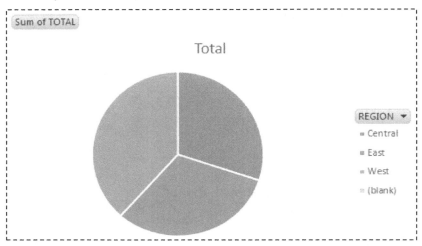

We now have our Dashboard data, but the format does not look very user friendly. Our next steps will focus on formatting & presentation.

Sum of TOTAL	Column Labe ▼					
Row Labels ▼	January	February	March	April	(blank)	Grand Total
Central	11358.9	19352.24	34097.239	73763.00053		138571.3795
East	3864.5283	19343.1909	38810.8125	83569.43715		145587.9689
West	2231.42423	18472.41947	38170.24125	110703.5915		169577.6765
(blank)						
Grand Total	17454.85253	57167.85037	111078.2928	268036.0292		453737.0248

Row Labels ▼	Sum of APPLES	Sum of ORANGES	Sum of MANGOS	Sum of TOTAL		Row Labels ▼	Sum of TOTAL
Central	43480.80136	53278.35597	41812.22219	138571.3795		Central	138571.3795
East	50625.74293	47117.44827	47844.77765	145587.9689		East	145587.9689
West	60697.03378	56037.4377	52843.20497	169577.6765		West	169577.6765
(blank)						(blank)	
Grand Total	154803.5781	156433.2419	142500.2048	453737.0248		Grand Total	453737.0248

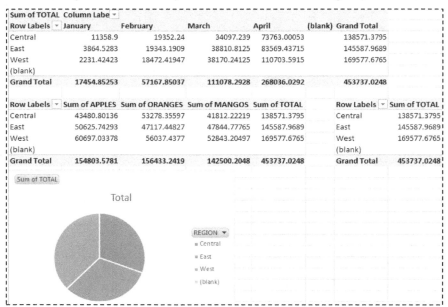

1. We'll begin with the pie chart, click on the chart, the **'PIVOTCHART TOOLS'** toolbar should appear

2. Select the **'DESIGN'** tab

3. Click the drop-down for **'Quick Layout'**

4. Select **'Layout 1'**

5. Change the chart title from **'TOTAL'** to **'% OF SALES BY REGION'**

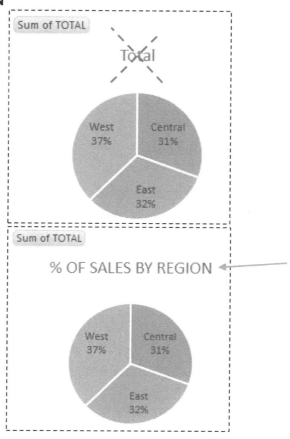

6. Change the **Row Labels** to **'REGION'**

7. Change the **Column Label** to **' MONTH'**

8. Change **'Sum of TOTAL'** to **'SALES'**

9. Remove the word **'Grand'** from **'Grand Total'** and change to uppercase

10. Add the word **'SALES'** after each *fruit*

11. Remove the words **'Sum of'** before each *fruit*

12. Center the row and column labels

13. Change the format for the sales results to currency, zero decimal places

Sum of TOTAL	Column Labe ▾					
Row Labels ▾	January	February	March	April	(blank)	Grand Total
Central	11358.9	19352.24	34097.239	73763.00053		138571.3795
East	3864.5283	19343.1909	38810.8125	83569.43715		145587.9689
West	2231.42423	18472.41947	38170.24125	110703.5915		169577.6765
(blank)						
Grand Total	17454.85253	57167.85037	111078.2928	268036.0292		453737.0248

Row Labels ▾	Sum of APPLES	Sum of ORANGES	Sum of MANGOS	Sum of TOTAL		Row Labels ▾	Sum of TOTAL
Central	43480.80136	53278.35597	41812.22219	138571.3795		Central	138571.3795
East	50625.74293	47117.44827	47844.77765	145587.9689		East	145587.9689
West	60697.03378	56037.4377	52843.20497	169577.6765		West	169577.6765
(blank)						(blank)	
Grand Total	154803.5781	156433.2419	142500.2048	453737.0248		Grand Total	453737.0248

After steps 6 -13 above:

SALES	MONTH ▾					
REGION ▾	January	February	March	April	(blank)	TOTAL
Central	$11,359	$19,352	$34,097	$73,763		$138,571
East	$3,865	$19,343	$38,811	$83,569		$145,588
West	$2,231	$18,472	$38,170	$110,704		$169,578
(blank)						
TOTAL	$17,455	$57,168	$111,078	$268,036		$453,737

REGION ▾	APPLES SALES	ORANGES SALES	MANGOS SALES	SALES		REGION ▾	SALES
Central	$43,481	$53,278	$41,812	$138,571		Central	$138,571
East	$50,626	$47,117	$47,845	$145,588		East	$145,588
West	$60,697	$56,037	$52,843	$169,578		West	$169,578
(blank)						(blank)	
TOTAL	$154,804	$156,433	$142,500	$453,737		Total	$453,737

While the formatting changes have improved the look of the Dashboard, let's take it a few steps further.

1. From the toolbar select the **'VIEW'** tab and uncheck the **'Gridlines'** box

2. Click cell **'A3'**, and then from the PIVOTTABLE TOOLS toolbar select the tab **DESIGN : PivotTable Styles**

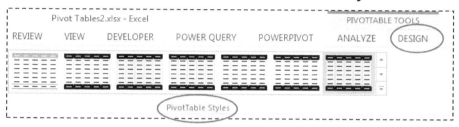

3. Select a format style you like

4. Repeat steps 2 & 3 for PivotTables in cells **'A11'** & 'G11'

5. In cell **'A1'** enter the text **'Monthly Sales Dashboard'** and merge across columns, so it appears centered over the data

6. Increase the font size of **'A1'** to 30 and bold

The results should now look similar to the following:

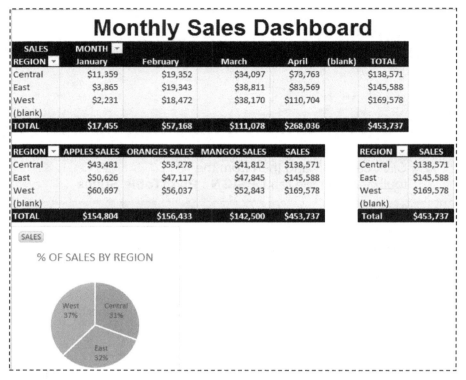

Almost done, lastly, let's hide the **(blank)** column and rows from display

7. Click the drop-down arrow for **'REGION'** in cell **'A4'**

8. Uncheck the **'(blank)'** check box

9. Click the **'OK'** button

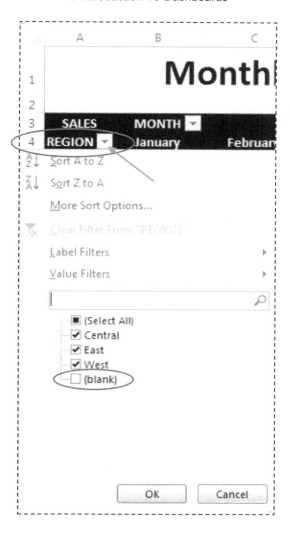

10. Repeat steps 7-9 for cells **'A11'** & **'G11'**

We now have a nicely formatted Dashboard:

Monthly Sales Dashboard

SALES	MONTH				
REGION	January	February	March	April	TOTAL
Central	$11,359	$19,352	$34,097	$73,763	$138,571
East	$3,865	$19,343	$38,811	$83,569	$145,588
West	$2,231	$18,472	$38,170	$110,704	$169,578
TOTAL	$17,455	$57,168	$111,078	$268,036	$453,737

REGION	APPLES SALES	ORANGES SALES	MANGOS SALES	SALES
Central	$43,481	$53,278	$41,812	$138,571
East	$50,626	$47,117	$47,845	$145,588
West	$60,697	$56,037	$52,843	$169,578
TOTAL	$154,804	$156,433	$142,500	$453,737

REGION	SALES
Central	$138,571
East	$145,588
West	$169,578
Total	$453,737

SALES

% OF SALES BY REGION

West 37% / Central 31% / East 32%

☑ Additional Information:

Depending on your audience, you may want to consider *protecting* your Dashboard to prevent unauthorized users from modifying it. As well as, *hide* any data source tabs, allowing your customers to see only the Dashboard itself.

1. To *hide* the **'Monthly Fruit Sales'** tab, **right click** over the tab and select **'Hide'**

2. To *unhide* **right click** over any tab and select **'Unhide'** *(the unhide option will become active once a tab is hidden)*

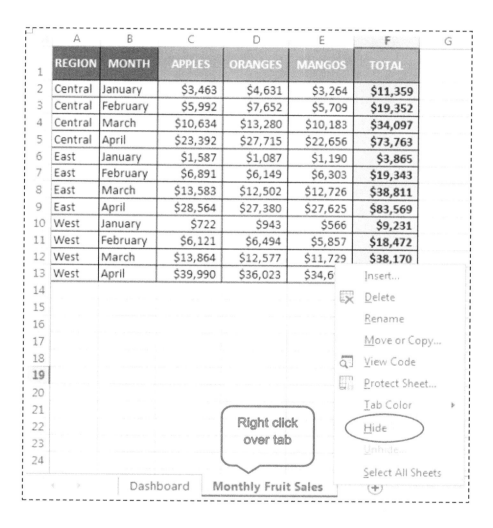

	A	B	C	D	E	F	G
1	REGION	MONTH	APPLES	ORANGES	MANGOS	TOTAL	
2	Central	January	$3,463	$4,631	$3,264	$11,359	
3	Central	February	$5,992	$7,652	$5,709	$19,352	
4	Central	March	$10,634	$13,280	$10,183	$34,097	
5	Central	April	$23,392	$27,715	$22,656	$73,763	
6	East	January	$1,587	$1,087	$1,190	$3,865	
7	East	February	$6,891	$6,149	$6,303	$19,343	
8	East	March	$13,583	$12,502	$12,726	$38,811	
9	East	April	$28,564	$27,380	$27,625	$83,569	
10	West	January	$722	$943	$566	$9,231	
11	West	February	$6,121	$6,494	$5,857	$18,472	
12	West	March	$13,864	$12,577	$11,729	$38,170	
13	West	April	$39,990	$36,023	$34,6		

Right click over tab

Insert...
Delete
Rename
Move or Copy...
View Code
Protect Sheet...
Tab Color ▸
Hide
Unhide...
Select All Sheets

Dashboard   Monthly Fruit Sales

To protect the Dashboard or any other tab:

3. From the toolbar ribbon select **'HOME'** and click the **'Format'** drop-down box

4. Select **'Protect Sheet...'**

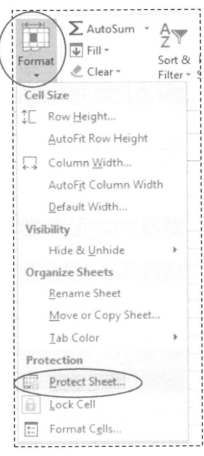

The following dialogue box will appear:

5. You may enter a password or leave blank *(if you enter a password, make sure at least one other person has access to it. They can serve as a backup resource, when you're unavailable)*

6. A good best practice is to leave the first two check boxes selected *(these will allow your customers to click on cells and scroll, but not change any content):*
    a. Select locked cells
    b. Select unlocked cells

7. Click the **'OK'** button

If a user tries to modify the sheet, they will receive the following message:

8. To **unprotect**, from the ribbon toolbar select **'HOME'** and click the **'Format'** drop-down box

9. Select **'Unprotect Sheet...'** *(this option will become available if a sheet is protected)*

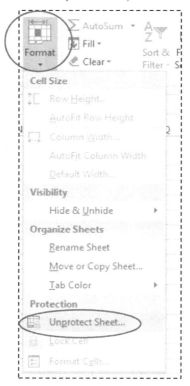

In the next chapter, we will look at how to update (Refresh) the Dashboard with new data, without having to re-create it.

CHAPTER 4
UPDATING EXISTING PIVOT TABLES WITH NEW OR MODIFIED DATA

If you have already created a Pivot Table or Dashboard where the layout and format is to your liking and you receive new or modified data, you can simply **Refresh** the data in your Pivot Table(s) without having to recreate them. To do this, you must:

1. Have correctly updated your Pivot Table settings to ensure your formatting does not change with new data

2. Ensure your existing Pivot Table is reading the correct data source *AND* cell range

Scenario:
You've spent a lot of time creating a monthly sales Dashboard and your customers like the format. You now would like to add new data (months) to this existing Dashboard, without having to recreate all of the Pivot Tables.

Detailed Example How To Use The Feature:
First, we want to make sure your Pivot Table formatting stays intact:

1. Make sure the Dashboard tab is **'Unprotected'**

2. From the toolbar select PIVOTTABLE TOOLS and the tab **ANALYZE**

3. Under **'PivotTable Name'** click the **'Options'** drop-down box and select **'Options'**

The following dialogue box will appear:

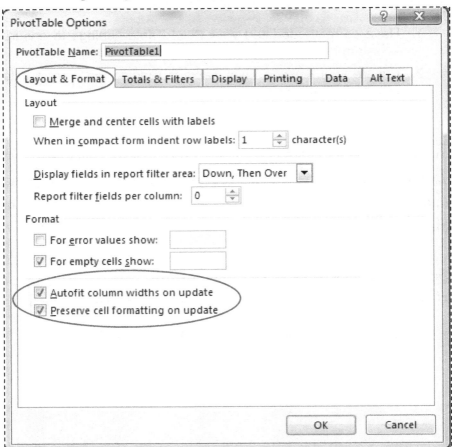

4. Select the **'Layout & Format'** tab
5. Click the last two check boxes:
   a. **<u>A</u>utofit** column widths on update
   b. **<u>P</u>reserve** cell formatting on update
6. Click the **'OK'** button

You will need to repeat steps 2-6 for each Pivot Table you've created

---

Next, verify your Pivot Table **data source** is correct:

1. Make sure the **Dashboard** tab is **'Unprotected'**
2. From the toolbar select PIVOTTABLE TOOLS and the tab **ANALYZE**
3. Click the drop-down box **'Change Data Source'** and select **'Change <u>D</u>ata Source...'**

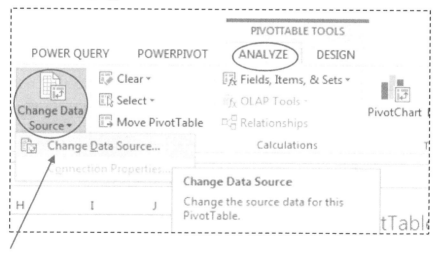

The following dialogue box will appear:

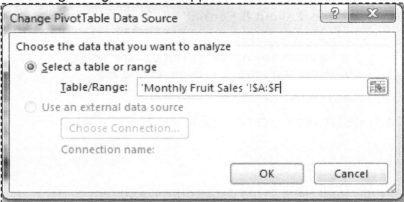

4. Verify the Table/Range is correct **_Note:_** _you will not receive an error message if the_ **_Range_** _is incorrect, however, the new data WILL NOT APPEAR on your Pivot Table / Dashboard._

Next, we will add new data to the Dashboard

Sample data to update (Refresh) the Pivot Table

	A	B	C	D	E	F
1	REGION	MONTH	APPLES	ORANGES	MANGOS	TOTAL
2	Central	January	$3,463	$4,631	$3,264	$11,359
3	Central	February	$5,992	$7,652	$5,709	$19,352
4	Central	March	$10,634	$13,280	$10,183	$34,097
5	Central	April	$23,392	$27,715	$22,656	$73,763
6	East	January	$1,587	$1,087	$1,190	$3,865
7	East	February	$6,891	$6,149	$6,303	$19,343
8	East	March	$13,583	$12,502	$12,726	$38,811
9	East	April	$28,564	$27,380	$27,625	$83,569
10	West	January	$722	$943	$566	$2,231
11	West	February	$6,121	$6,494	$5,857	$18,472
12	West	March	$13,864	$12,577	$11,729	$38,170
13	West	April	$39,990	$36,023	$34,691	$110,704
14	East	May	$29,964	$30,380	$28,125	$88,469
15	Central	May	$26,492	$29,215	$25,756	$81,463
16	West	May	$41,990	$38,473	$36,591	$117,054

1. Click cell **'A3'**

2. From the toolbar select PIVOTTABLE TOOLS and the tab **ANALYZE**

3. Click the drop-down box **'Refresh'** and select **'Refresh All'**

Note: _selecting the_ **_'Refresh'_** _option would only update the_ **_active_** _Pivot Table, by selecting_ **_'Refresh All'_** _we're updating all of the Pivot Tables in the Dashboard._

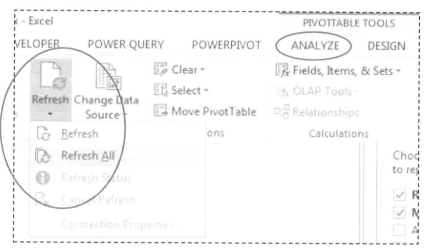

We now have the May sales data added to the Dashboard:

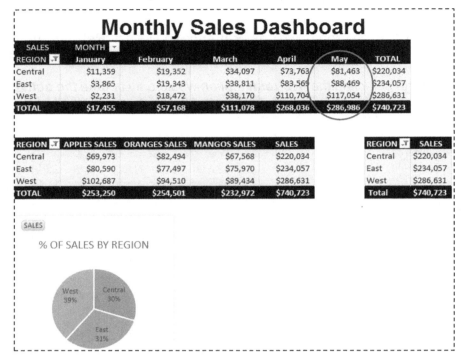

In the next two chapters (5 & 6) we will review helpful formulas to assist in troubleshooting some common data formatting issues with Pivot Tables.

CHAPTER 5
FORMULA = LEN

Formula:
- LEN

Definition:
- Counts the number characters in a cell

Quick Example:

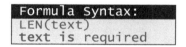

Formula Syntax:
LEN(text)
text is required

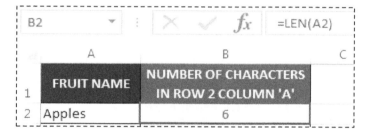

Scenario:

You've been given an report that was created by a Data Base Administrator (DBA). The DBA created the file by running a query in a database, exporting the results into a .CSV file, and then opened and re-saved the report as an Excel® file.

As the Business Analyst, you're attempting to reconcile the data using a Pivot Table. In your analysis, you've discovered cell values that *"look"* to be the same, but are being returned as two separate records in your results.

You use the LEN function to troubleshoot why you're getting two separate records in your results for what appear to be the same value.

Detailed Example How To Use The Formula:

Pivot table results, the fruit '**Apples**' is listed twice and should only be listed once:

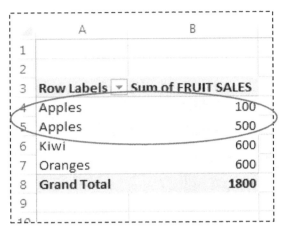

Sample data

To download a free copy of the Excel® file used in this scenario please go to:
http://bentonexcelbooks.my-free.website/sample-data-files
select the file for Chapters 5 & 6 (once open select the LEN tab) in the 'The Step-By-Step Guide To Pivot Tables & Introduction to Dashboards' section.

	A	B
1	**FRUIT NAME**	**FRUIT SALES**
2	Apples	100
3	Kiwi	100
4	Oranges	100
5	Apples	200
6	Kiwi	200
7	Oranges	200
8	Apples	300
9	Kiwi	300
10	Oranges	300
11		

1. You begin by sorting the results by 'Fruit Name' in Ascending order

2. Add a column, in cell '**C1**' label it "**LEN FUNCTION**"

3. Next apply the '**LEN**' function for 'Fruit Name' in cell '**C2**'

	A	B	C
1	**FRUIT NAME**	**FRUIT SALES**	**LEN FUNCTION**
2	Apples	100	
3	Apples	200	
4	Apples	300	
5	Kiwi	100	
6	Kiwi	200	
7	Kiwi	300	
8	Oranges	100	
9	Oranges	200	
10	Oranges	300	
11			

4. From the toolbar select **Formulas : Insert Function**

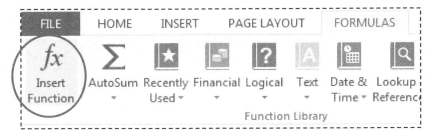

5. Type "**LEN**" in the **'Search for a function:'** dialogue box

6. Click the '**Go**' button

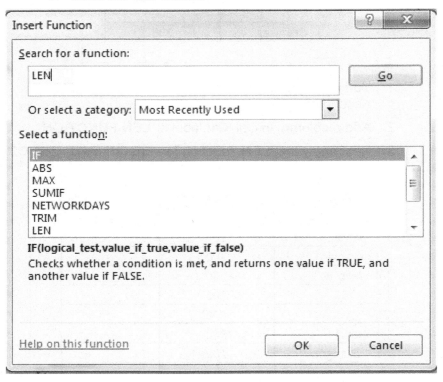

The following should now appear:

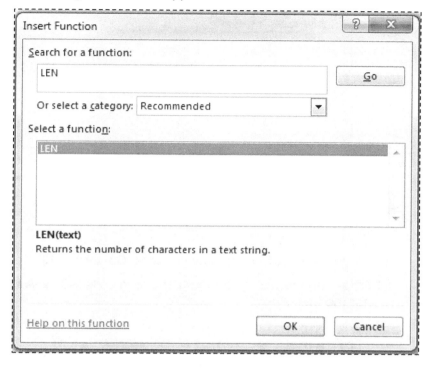

7. Click the '**OK**' button

8. Click on cell '**A2**' or enter '**A2**' in the dialogue box

9. Click 'the '**OK**' button

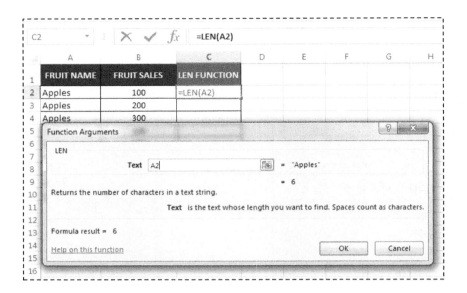

10. Copy the LEN formula down to cells '**C3**' thru '**C10**'

11. There appears to be an extra space in cells '**A3**' & '**A4**' for the fruit *'Apple'*

	A	B	C
1	**FRUIT NAME**	**FRUIT SALES**	**LEN FUNCTION**
2	Apples	100	6
3	Apples	200	7
4	Apples	300	7
5	Kiwi	100	4
6	Kiwi	200	4
7	Kiwi	300	4
8	Oranges	100	7
9	Oranges	200	7
10	Oranges	300	7

12. Remove the extra space in in cells "**A3**' & '**A4**' for the fruit 'Apple'

13. Save your changes

14. Re-run your Pivot Table

Results now appear correctly

	Row Labels ▾	Sum of FRUIT SALES
3		
4	Apples	600
5	Kiwi	600
6	Oranges	600
7	**Grand Total**	**1800**

CHAPTER 6
FORMULA = TRIM

Formula:
- TRIM

Definition:
- Removes all extraneous spaces from a cell, except for single spaces between words.

Quick Example:

```
Formula Syntax:
TRIM(text)
text is required
```

C2	▼	:	✕ ✓	fx	=TRIM(A2)	

	A	B	C	D
1	FRUIT NAME	LEN COUNT OF CHARACTERS	TRIM FUNCTION	LEN COUNT OF CHARACTERS
2	Apples, Bananas, Mangos	27	Apples, Bananas, Mangos	23
3	Apples, Bananas, Mangos	23	Apples, Bananas, Mangos	23
4				

Scenario:

You've been given a Excel® report generated by another application. Upon review you see the content in the cells contains extra spaces between and after the words. In order to make the report usable for analysis and presentation you need to remove the extraneous spaces.

Detailed Example How To Use The Formula:

Sample data:

To download a free copy of the Excel® file used in this scenario please go to:
http://bentonexcelbooks.my-free.website/sample-data-files select the file for **Chapters 5 & 6** *(once open select the* **TRIM tab)** *in the* **'The Step-By-Step Guide To Pivot Tables & Introduction to Dashboards'** *section*

	A	B
1	FRUIT NAME	LEN COUNT OF CHARACTERS
2	Apples, Bananas, Mangos	27
3	Apples, Bananas, Mangos	23
4	Kiwi, Oranges, Strawberries	27
5	Kiwi, Oranges, Strawberries	29
6	Blueberries, Raspberries, Blackberries	38
7	Blueberries, Raspberries, Blackberries	40

1. Add a column, in cell '**C1**' label it "**TRIM FUNCTION**"

2. Next, apply the '**TRIM**' function for 'Fruit Name' in row '**C2**'

	A	B	C
1	FRUIT NAME	LEN COUNT OF CHARACTERS	TRIM FUNCTION
2	Apples, Bananas, Mangos	27	
3	Apples, Bananas, Mangos	23	
4	Kiwi, Oranges, Strawberries	27	
5	Kiwi, Oranges, Strawberries	29	
6	Blueberries, Raspberries, Blackberries	38	
7	Blueberries, Raspberries, Blackberries	40	

3. From the toolbar select **Formulas : Insert Function**

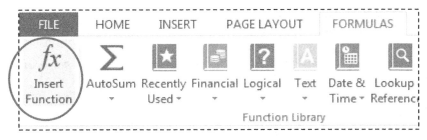

4. Type "**TRIM**" in the 'Search for a function:' dialogue box

5. Click the '**Go**' button

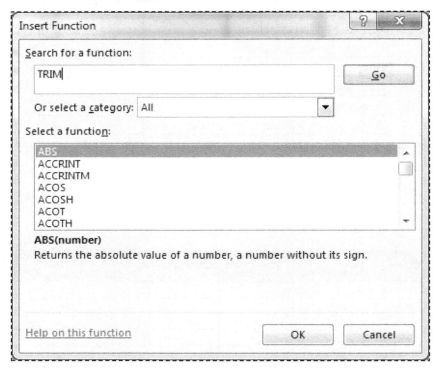

The following should now appear:

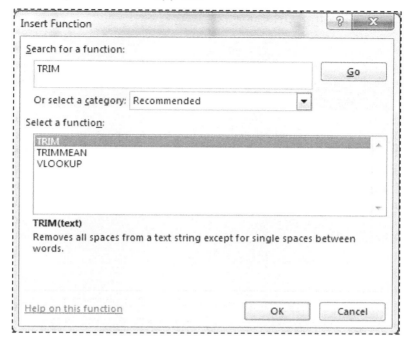

6. Click the '**OK**' button

7. Click cell '**A2**' or enter '**A2**' in the dialogue box

8. Click the '**OK**' button

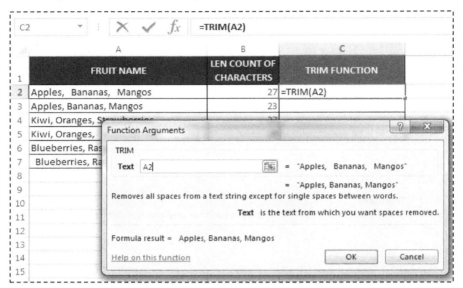

9. Copy the **TRIM** formula down cells '**C3**' thru '**C7**'

10. The extra spaces have been removed

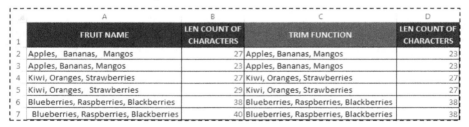

Next we'll copy and paste as a value the contents of column C and remove the columns (B, C, & D) used for troubleshooting.

11. Highlight cells '**C2**' thru '**C7**'

12. Click the '**Copy**' button or **CTL+C** from your keyboard

13. Select cell '**A2**'

14. Right click and select '**Paste Special…**'

15. Select the '**<u>V</u>alues**' radio button

16. Click the '**OK**' button

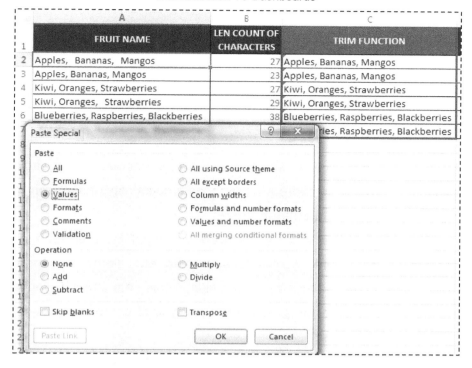

A	B	C
FRUIT NAME	**LEN COUNT OF CHARACTERS**	**TRIM FUNCTION**
Apples, Bananas, Mangos	27	Apples, Bananas, Mangos
Apples, Bananas, Mangos	23	Apples, Bananas, Mangos
Kiwi, Oranges, Strawberries	27	Kiwi, Oranges, Strawberries
Kiwi, Oranges, Strawberries	29	Kiwi, Oranges, Strawberries
Blueberries, Raspberries, Blackberries	38	Blueberries, Raspberries, Blackberries

17. Highlight columns **'B'**, **'C'**, & **'D'**

18. Right click and select **'Delete'**, the troubleshooting columns **'B'**, **'C'**, & **'D'** should now be removed

We have successfully removed all extraneous spaces from records contained in **column 'A'**. Further analysis and reporting can be completed without error.

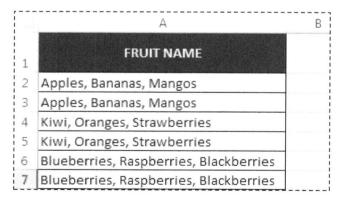

A	B
FRUIT NAME	
Apples, Bananas, Mangos	
Apples, Bananas, Mangos	
Kiwi, Oranges, Strawberries	
Kiwi, Oranges, Strawberries	
Blueberries, Raspberries, Blackberries	
Blueberries, Raspberries, Blackberries	

CHAPTER 7
PIVOT TABLES (ADVANCED)

In chapter 2 we reviewed some basic and intermediate Pivot Table examples, now let's explore the advanced functionality of **'Grouping'** data and inserting **'Calculated Fields'**.

When you have a lot of detailed individual records such as customer demographics, sales, location data, etc. Sometimes more insight can be gained when you can cluster this data into categories or ranges. The **'Grouping'** feature allows you to complete this type of segmented analysis.

Additionally, the type of work you perform may require more complex or technical types of calculations than those included in the standard set of Pivot Table 'Value Field Settings.' This is when being able to insert your own **'Calculated Fields'** is particularly helpful.

Scenario:
You've received a large amount of detailed customer records and need to:

1. Group the number of customers by how much they spent, and include their segment's percentage to the overall sales total.

Detailed Example How To Use The Feature:

Sample data, due to space limitations **the entire data set is not displayed**:

To download a free copy of the Excel® file used in this scenario please go to:
http://bentonexcelbooks.my-free.website/sample-data-files
select the file for Chapter 7 (Grouping) in the **'The Step-By-Step Guide To Pivot Tables & Introduction to Dashboards'** *section*

	A CUSTOMER ID	B AMOUNT PURCHASED
1		
2	111	$ 142
3	222	$ 153
4	333	$ 442
5	444	$ 409
6	555	$ 136
7	666	$ 147
8	777	$ 436
9	888	$ 403
10	999	$ 1,500
11	1110	$ 106
12	1221	$ 395
13	1332	$ 362
14	1443	$ 857
15	1554	$ 890
16	1665	$ 1,157
17	1776	$ 1,146
18	1887	$ 719
19	1998	$ 796
20	2109	$ 1,019
21	2220	$ 1,052
22	2331	$ 100
23	2442	$ 277
24	2553	$ 385
25	2664	$ 533
26	2775	$ 100
27	2886	$ 401
28	2997	$ 400
29	3108	$ 657
30	3219	$ 985

1. Insert a Pivot Table, please see the beginning of chapter 2 if you do not already know how to create a new Pivot Table.

Please select **columns 'A1' – 'B31'** for your **Table/Range**.

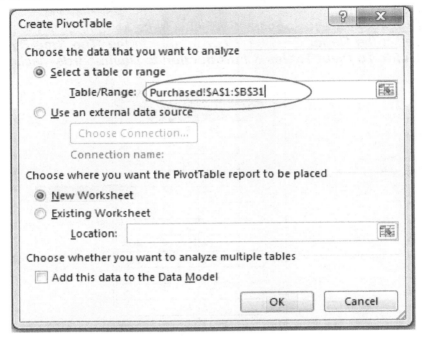

2. Select **'AMOUNT PURCHASED'** and drag under the **'ROWS'**
section of the **PivotTable Fields** dialogue box

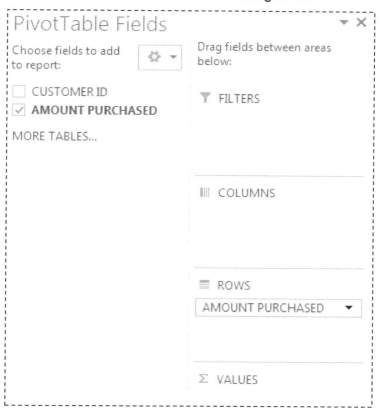

3. Select **'CUSTOMER ID'** _twice_ and drag under the **'VALUES'** section of the **PivotTable Fields** dialogue box.

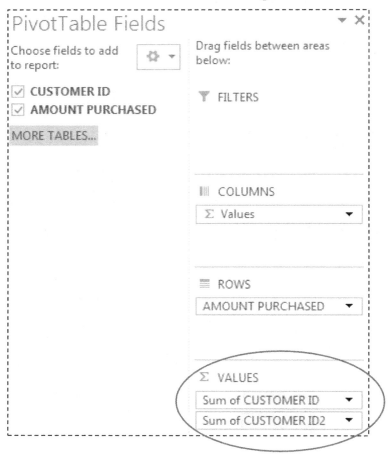

The following should now be displayed:

	A	B	C
3	Row Labels ▾	Sum of CUSTOMER ID	Sum of CUSTOMER ID2
4	$ 100	5106	5106
5	$ 106	1110	1110
6	$ 136	555	555
7	$ 142	111	111
8	$ 147	666	666
9	$ 153	222	222
10	$ 277	2442	2442
11	$ 362	1332	1332
12	$ 385	2553	2553
13	$ 395	1221	1221
14	$ 400	2997	2997
15	$ 401	2886	2886
16	$ 403	888	888
17	$ 409	444	444
18	$ 436	777	777
19	$ 442	333	333
20	$ 533	2664	2664
21	$ 657	3108	3108
22	$ 719	1887	1887
23	$ 752	3330	3330
24	$ 796	1998	1998
25	$ 857	1443	1443
26	$ 890	1554	1554
27	$ 985	3219	3219
28	$ 1,019	2109	2109
29	$ 1,052	2220	2220
30	$ 1,146	1776	1776
31	$ 1,157	1665	1665
32	$ 1,500	999	999
33	Grand Total	51615	51615

4. Click cell '**A4**'.

5. From the toolbar select PIVOTTABLE TOOLS and the tab **ANALYZE**

6. Select **'Group Field'**

The following dialogue box will appear:

7. Click both the **'Starting at:'** and **'Ending at:'** check boxes

8. **'Starting at:'** will default to 100 (this is the *lowest value* in the dataset)

9. **'Ending at:'** will default to 1500 (this is the *highest value* in the dataset)

10. Enter 100 in the '**By:**' field *(this is the amount between group segments)*

11. Click the **'OK'** button

We've now grouped customer purchase amounts into ~$100 segments, with each bracket differential representing approximately $100:

100-199
200-299
300-399
400-499
500-599
600-699
700-799
800-899
900-999
1000-1099
1100-1199
1400-1500

	Row Labels	Sum of CUSTOMER ID	Sum of CUSTOMER ID2
3			
4	100-199	7770	7770
5	200-299	2442	2442
6	300-399	5106	5106
7	400-499	8325	8325
8	500-599	2664	2664
9	600-699	3108	3108
10	700-799	7215	7215
11	800-899	2997	2997
12	900-999	3219	3219
13	1000-1099	4329	4329
14	1100-1199	3441	3441
15	1400-1500	999	999
16	**Grand Total**	**51615**	**51615**

However, this table is not providing meaningful information, because it is incorrectly summing **'CUSTOMER ID'**, to fix this:

12. In the PivotTable Fields list, in the **'VALUES'** section, click the drop-down box for the *first* **'Sum of CUSTOMER ID'**

13. Select the **'Value Field Settings...'**option.

The following dialogue box will appear:

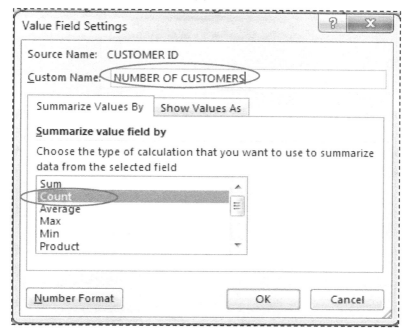

1. In the **'Custom Name:'** field change to **'NUMBER OF CUSTOMERS'**

2. In the **'Summarize value field by'** list box select **'Count'**.

3. Click the **'OK'** button

Next, we'll address the *second* **'Sum of CUSTOMER ID'** field

4. In the **PivotTable Fields** list, in the **'VALUES'** section, click the drop-down box for the *second* **'Sum of CUSTOMER ID'**

5. Select the **'Value Field Settings...'** option

The following dialogue box will appear:

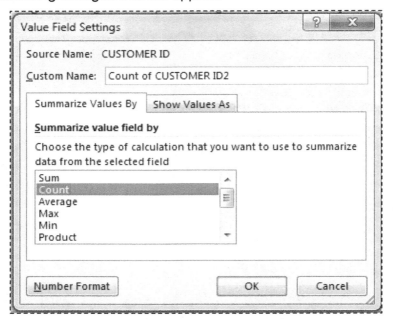

6. In the **'Custom Name:'** field change to '**% OF CUSTOMERS**'

7. In the **'Summarize value field by'** list select **'Count'**

8. Click the **'Show Values As'** tab

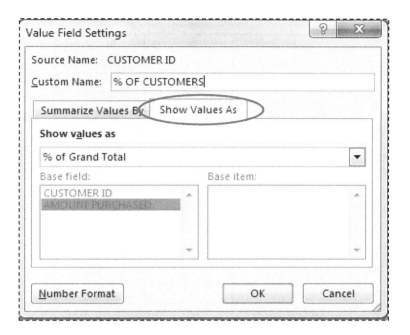

9. Click the **'Show values as'** drop-down box and select **'% of Grand Total'**

10. Click the **'OK'** button

11. Change the label in cell '**A3**' to '**AMOUNT PURCHASED**'

We now have a report that groups the number of customers by how much they spent and the segment's percentage to overall total sales.

	AMOUNT PURCHASE[▾	NUMBER OF CUSTOMERS	% OF CUSTOMERS
3			
4	100-199	7	23%
5	200-299	1	3%
6	300-399	3	10%
7	400-499	6	20%
8	500-599	1	3%
9	600-699	1	3%
10	700-799	3	10%
11	800-899	2	7%
12	900-999	1	3%
13	1000-1099	2	7%
14	1100-1199	2	7%
15	1400-1500	1	3%
16	Grand Total	30	100%

For our last example, we'll examine inserting calculated fields into a Pivot Table.

Scenario:

You're responsible for analyzing your company's store sales data plan vs. actual. This is something you do every month and it is the type of business, where some stores may close and others open from month-to-month. You need to report:

1. The sales dollar variance -/+ plan vs. actual
2. The percent variance -/+ plan vs. actual

Sample data:

	A	B	C
1	**STORE**	**PLAN SALES**	**ACTUAL SALES**
2	AAA	$ 50,000	$ 55,000
3	BBB	$ 40,000	$ 35,500
4	CCC	$ 30,000	$ 32,000
5	DDD	$ 20,000	$ 18,500
6	EEE	$ 25,000	$ 42,000

1. Create a Pivot Table, make sure to select the entire column of '**A**' – '**C**' for the **Table/Range**. This is what will allow us to simply refresh the data each month, when new stores are opened and others close

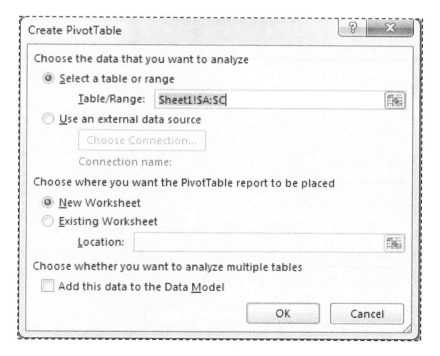

2. Select '**STORE**' and drag under the '**ROWS**' section of the **PivotTable Fields** list

3. Select '**PLAN SALES**' and drag under the '**VALUES**' section of the **PivotTable Fields** list

93

4. Select **'ACTUAL SALES'** and drag under the **'VALUES'** section of the **PivotTable Fields** dialogue box

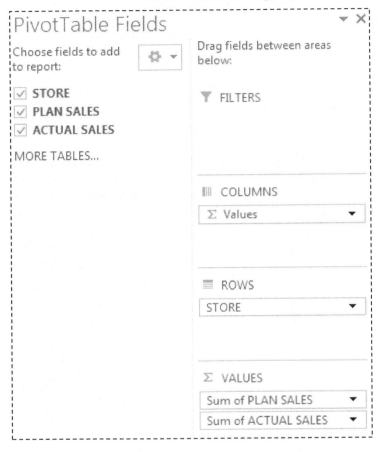

5. Change the label in cell **'A3'** to '**STORE'**

6. Change the label in cell **'B3'** to '**PLN SALES'**

7. Change the label in cell **'C3'** to '**ACT SALES'**

8. Change the formatting in cells **'B4'** – **'C9'** to currency, with no decimal places

The Pivot Table should look *similar* to the following:

	A	B	C
1			
2			
3	STORE ▾	PLN SALES	ACT SALES
4	AAA	$ 50,000	$ 55,000
5	BBB	$ 40,000	$ 35,500
6	CCC	$ 30,000	$ 32,000
7	DDD	$ 20,000	$ 18,500
8	EEE	$ 25,000	$ 42,000
9	(blank)		
10	Grand Total	$ 165,000	$ 183,000

Next, we will add our first calculated field that shows the sales dollar variance -/+ plan vs. actual.

9. From the toolbar select PIVOTTABLE TOOLS and the tab **ANALYZE**

10. Click the **'Fields, Items & Sets'** drop-down box

11. Select **'Calculated Field…'**

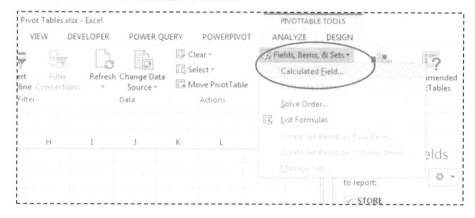

The following dialogue box will appear:

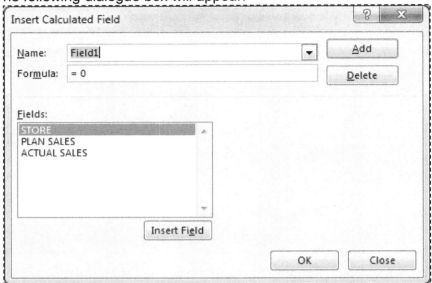

12. In the **Name:** field enter **'Dollars -/+ plan vs actual'**

13. In the **Formula:** field delete the zero '0', but leave the equal '=' sign

14. Select **'ACTUAL SALES'** from the **'Fields'** list and click the **'Insert Field'** button

15. Add the minus '-' symbol in the **Formula:** field after **'ACTUAL SALES'**

16. Select **'PLAN SALES'** from the **'Fields'** list and click the **'Insert Field'** button

This formula should now be in the **Formula:** field

```
='ACTUAL SALES' -'PLAN SALES'
```

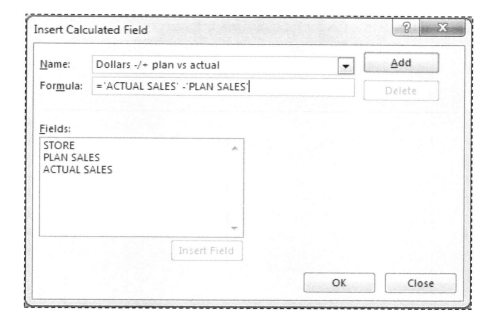

17. Click the **'OK'** button

The following field was added to our PivotTable results:

STORE ▼	PLN SALES	ACT SALES	Sum of Dollars -/+ plan vs actual
AAA	$ 50,000	$ 55,000	$ 5,000
BBB	$ 40,000	$ 35,500	$ (4,500)
CCC	$ 30,000	$ 32,000	$ 2,000
DDD	$ 20,000	$ 18,500	$ (1,500)
EEE	$ 25,000	$ 42,000	$ 17,000
(blank)			$ -
Grand Total	$ 165,000	$ 183,000	$ 18,000

Now, we'll add the percent variance -/+ plan vs. actual

1. From the toolbar select PIVOTTABLE TOOLS and the tab **ANALYZE**

2. Click the **'Fields, Items & Sets'** drop-down box

3. Select **'Calculated Field...'**

The following dialogue box will appear:

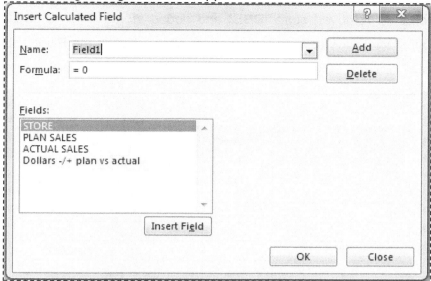

Note: *the calculated field* **'Dollars -/+ plan vs actual'** *has been added to our list of available* **'Fields:'.**

4. In the **Name:** field enter **'Percent -/+ plan vs actual'**

5. In the **Formula:** field delete the zero '0', but leave the equal '=' sign

6. Add the below formula to the **Formula:** field
   `=('ACTUAL SALES'- 'PLAN SALES')/ 'PLAN SALES'`

7. Click the **'OK'** button

The following field was added to our PivotTable results: ***Note:*** *we need to change the* **format to a percent (%)** *in the results*

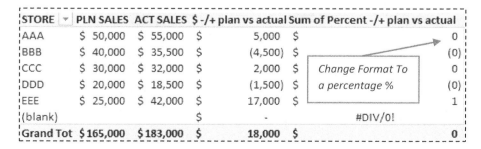

STORE ▾	PLN SALES	ACT SALES	$ -/+ plan vs actual	Sum of Percent -/+ plan vs actual
AAA	$ 50,000	$ 55,000	$ 5,000	$ 0
BBB	$ 40,000	$ 35,500	$ (4,500)	$ (0)
CCC	$ 30,000	$ 32,000	$ 2,000	$ 0
DDD	$ 20,000	$ 18,500	$ (1,500)	$ (0)
EEE	$ 25,000	$ 42,000	$ 17,000	$ 1
(blank)			$ -	#DIV/0!
Grand Tot	$ 165,000	$ 183,000	$ 18,000	$ 0

Change Format To a percentage %

Let's examine now how our results change when we *add* or *remove* stores. I removed store **'BBB'** and added stores **'FFF'** & **'GGG'**, notice where the **(blank)** row appears after I refresh the Pivot Table data? *Please see **chapter 4** for instructions on how to refresh Pivot Table data.*

STORE ▼	PLN SALES	ACT SALES	$ -/+ plan vs actual	% -/+ plan vs actual
AAA	$ 50,000	$ 55,000	$ 5,000	10.0%
CCC	$ 30,000	$ 32,000	$ 2,000	6.7%
DDD	$ 20,000	$ 18,500	$ (1,500)	-7.5%
EEE	$ 25,000	$ 42,000	$ 17,000	68.0%
(blank)			$ -	#DIV/0!
FFF	$ 25,000	$ 22,000	$ (3,000)	-12.0%
GGG	$ 25,000	$ 24,000	$ (1,000)	-4.0%
Total	$175,000	$193,500	$ 18,500	10.6%

To resolve this, I'm going to change the **'STORE'** *field sorting options to '**S**ort A to Z'*. This will ensure each time I refresh the data in the future, my results will always be in Ascending order.

STORE ↕	PLN SALES	ACT SALES	$ -/+ plan vs actual	% -/+ plan vs actual
AAA	$ 50,000	$ 55,000	$ 5,000	10.0%
CCC	$ 30,000	$ 32,000	$ 2,000	6.7%
DDD	$ 20,000	$ 18,500	$ (1,500)	-7.5%
EEE	$ 25,000	$ 42,000	$ 17,000	68.0%
FFF	$ 25,000	$ 22,000	$ (3,000)	-12.0%
GGG	$ 25,000	$ 24,000	$ (1,000)	-4.0%
(blank)			$ -	#DIV/0!
Total	$175,000	$193,500	$ 18,500	10.6%

*To hide the **(blank)** row from display see page 54 for instructions.*

To remove or change a calculated field:

1. From the toolbar select PIVOTTABLE TOOLS and the tab **ANALYZE**

2. Click the **'Fields, Items & Sets'** drop-down box

3. Select **'Calculated Field...'**

The following dialogue box will appear:

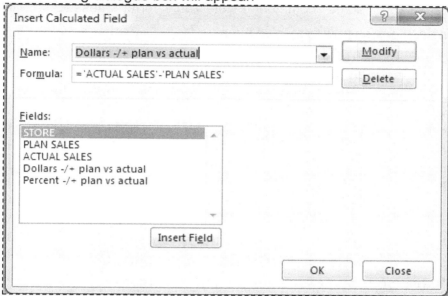

4. In the **'Name:'** drop-down box select the calculated field you would like to change or remove

5. Click appropriate button, either **'Modify'** or **'Delete'**

CHAPTER 8
PIVOT TABLE ERROR MESSAGES & HOW TO
RESOLVE THEM

Below are some common Pivot Table error messages with instructions on how to resolve them.

Note: *The following is not a comprehensive list of all the Pivot Table error messages, just a few of the more common ones.*

Error message:

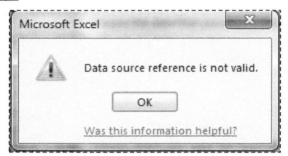

'Data source reference is not valid.'

Typically appears when you attempt to create a Pivot Table, with a **blank header row**.

To resolve, delete the blank row (in this case row 1) or make sure you select the correct header rows and supporting data before clicking **Insert : Pivot Table** from the toolbar.

<u>Error message</u>:

'We can't make this change for the selected cells because it will affect a PivotTable. Use the field list to change the report. If you are trying to insert or delete cells, move the PivotTable and try again.'

Often appears when you attempt to delete a calculated field, row, or column. For example, you no longer want to see the row '**Grand Total**', unfortunately, you can't simply delete this row, you'll receive the above error message.

| 19 | 100 | $ | 10,339 | $ | 2,585 | 16 |
| 20 | Grand Total | $ | 480,946 | $ | 7,515 | |

To remove '**Grand Total**' rows and columns we need to change the Pivot Table design.

1. Click the cell you would like to remove and then from the toolbar select PIVOTTABLE TOOLS and the tab **DESIGN**

2. Click the drop-down box for '**Grand Totals**' and select your preferred option:
   a. O<u>f</u>f for Rows and Columns
   b. O<u>n</u> for Rows and Columns
   c. On for <u>R</u>ows Only
   d. On for <u>C</u>olumns Only

For this example, we will select '**O<u>f</u>f for Rows and Columns**'

The **'Grand Total'** row has now been removed.

| 19 | 100 | $ | 10,339 | $ | 2,585 | 16 |
| 20 | | | | | | |

A Message From The Author

Thank you for purchasing and reading this book! Your feedback is valued and appreciated! Please take a few minutes and leave a review.

Other Books Available By This Author:

1. The Step-By-Step Guide To The 25 Most Common Microsoft® Excel® Formulas & Features

2. The Step-By-Step Guide To The **VLOOKUP** formula in Microsoft® Excel®

3. The Microsoft® Excel® Step-By-Step Training Guide **Book Bundle**

58493849R00064

Made in the USA
Middletown, DE
07 August 2019